The Secret of Anti-Procrastination

Technique 10 Minutes A Day Eliminate Procrastination for

Easier, Happier and More Successful Lives

Table of Contents

Introduction

I came across a research study which revealed that one out of five people is considered a chronic procrastinator. This is quite alarming, but what's, even more, worse is the fact that the number has quadrupled in the last 30 years. But what is procrastination and why do some people some get alarmed with this fact?

Procrastination according to Oxford dictionary is "to delay or put off something until later."

So procrastination involves two significant factors: time and action which makes it meaningful to anyone for it can result to a wide range of life-altering issues including poor health, bad performance in the job or school, financial difficulties, and you could add more to this list. As we often say, time is valuable and time flew never to return.

When we choose to delay something that needs to be done, it's usually for one reason or another. But, had you ever consider impatience to be synonymous with procrastination? These two words seem too conflicting in meaning and character, but a study on procrastination and impatience published in the *Journal of Behavior and Experimental Economics* (Vol 29, 2015) disclosed that those people who are impatient are most likely to procrastinate.

In the conduct of the study, *Ernesto Reuben*, a behavioral economist involved a bunch of MBA students. These participants were offered a check they could cash right away, or if they can wait for two weeks more, then they can have a more prominent sum. What did most participants choose? More than 60% of these number of participants preferred instant cash over waiting for a larger amount. This is quite understandable, but what's surprising is when more than half of these people didn't cash out the check but waited for more than two weeks. In fact, 30% of those students who waited didn't cash out their checks in one month. It didn't sound logical coming from MA students when they could have been rewarded more for less time of waiting.

Chapter 1: Reasons Why People Procrastinate

I have come across the topic of procrastination too many times but have never given it much thought until now.

Since I could remember, I never acquired any good study habit in the course of my study. I merely love cramming in the sense that when I study a week or a day before my examination, nothing will get into my head. I got too distracted by too many things. However, an hour or minutes before the exam, before my teacher would come into the classroom, I would just scan my note and whoa! My eyes would serve as a scanning device that everything I have read was plastered all over my thinking. It's easy as that! This had continued for years until it was fully embedded in my senses.

This procrastination habit continued to be a part of me. When I'm working in the office, I will lay down everything - documents, writing pad, notes, record on my office table. Then I would do something else like opening my mailbox, calling someone on the phone, or order another cup of coffee. I would also leave my office to check on other workers. It's only after lunch that I would get back to what I plan to do for the day. Since I get fueled up late, I also got into this habit of staying late to do my job. While others are working from 8:00 to 5:00, my office hours extend up to 8:00 in the evening.

When I spread most of my things on my office table, I expect them to be as they were when I left them. When someone tried to arrange them, I could no longer find my way to where I left off. It would take me sometime before I could finally locate the point to where I should start.

Because of my being a procrastinator, I produced too much clutter in my life - in my job, my relationship, and in my life, and this includes mental confusion as well.

It's accepted that many of us do procrastinate once in awhile especially when we lack the drive to work on an assignment. We promise ourselves to work on it later or in the next day. There are times when we feel too lazy or too tired to do anything at all and postponing a task seems to be appropriate. However, before you knew it, you acquire a long list of pending tasks that need to be done in such short time.

Procrastination seems to be a normal part of a person's life, but it's a major reason why some people fail, and others get on top ahead of others. Procrastinating can get you at the end of the line when you can have the option to be on top. In other words, though procrastination seems to be as worthless as it seems, understanding how it affects your life can, in fact, lead you to success and a better life.

Why Do We Tend to Procrastinate

All along, people are aware that procrastination falls on the negative side of the balance of habits. Procrastination may buy you some time, but it usually ends up giving you stress and anxiety as well. Consider Mary, a student who got this habit of studying at the last hour or doing her assignments just before the time when it needs to be submitted. It's clear that aside from the anxiety she gets from trying to beat the deadline, the quality of work is not comparable to when she should have enough time to prepare.

Sense of Fear of Rejection

The usual common cause of procrastination is fear. It could either be fear of failure or fear of success. Either way, you got this sense of fear because you fear rejection.

Most people who have a deep-rooted fear of rejection feel that if they procrastinate, they can delay doing things that they are afraid of facing. Procrastination serves as a protection mechanism which one expects to shield him from facing a possible failure out of doing something.

By accepting the fact that failure is not as fatal as you think, you can get away from this threatening fear. Note that mistakes are reversible and you can always have the second chance to fix where it goes wrong. It's just a matter of setting your mind on positive things and getting away from negative thoughts that could repressed you from doing things right. Procrastination is never an answer to your problem of facing your fear. It only prolongs the agony. Try and try until you succeed!

Perfectionism

Perfectionism or too much of it can also be a cause of procrastination. Perfectionists do find it hard to take action on a job unless they can be sure it can do be done perfectly to their satisfaction. This mindset becomes a problem when you have something new to try out or when you will do something that is somehow different to whatever it is that you're used to. Because of this type of mindset, consciously or subconsciously, you are always worrying about whether you will be able to produce a satisfying end-result.

It's normal to be proud of anything you have done especially when you are trying to do your best. However, when your expectation becomes quite unrealistic, that what you want to complete is actually beyond what you can fulfill, then that's where the problem sets in. When you know that you can't do what you expect to do, it's easier to delay doing it until you can find a better idea to do something better, which often is not the case. The delay does not mean you can get away from doing it.

Such manner of perfectionism leads to procrastination as it encourages you to put off any attempt to do a certain task until the time when you think you can do it perfectly. This is almost near to having a fear of failure or rejection with the exception that it includes your worry of not being able to meet your high standard.

To resolve this issue of perfectionism, try to do your best but be contented and happy with the outcome. Although everyone is trying hard to perfection, consider that there is nothing perfect in this word!

The Lack of Energy

Having a low energy level or the lack of it is likewise a reason for procrastination. If you don't have the energy, then it follows that you don't feel like doing much at all. A poor diet coupled with insufficient sleep are lifestyle habits that won't improve your sense of vibrancy, and it pays a big factor on how you want to take action.

Being able to identify this problem is significant to get rid of your procrastination habit. If you intend to be active and productive, but don't have the energy to do, then it's clear that you are indeed suffering from low energy supply.

To cure this, you have to develop a healthy lifestyle.

- Have adequate amount of sleep
- Eat a healthy well-balanced diet
- Exercise regularly
- Have a regular physical check-up

The Lack of Direction in Life

People who simply don't have the focus often procrastinate. The lack of direction is the frequent cause why people tend to lose focus in life.

In life, we are motivated by various factors, and unless we recognize these factors that can drive us in the right direction, we can continue drifting. To set your point of direction, you need to set up a goal. This will motivate you to move in the certain direction to arrive at a certain end-point. Only then will you have a direction-oriented life.

Once you have a goal as your target, you will regain back your focus and your time, and your energy is likewise focused on the achievement of your goal. This way, you aren't mishandling your time and life!

In setting your goal, set them high enough to encourage you to take action. Make sure they are realistic to be attainable and inspiring to make you hopeful. Also, set a duration, as it can't go on forever. Goals are set along with time-specific and measurable objectives or tasks to keep you going day after day.

By keeping along with these objectives, you can get rid of procrastination.

Reasons to Getting Rid of this Delaying Tactic!

Procrastination is a trap you can't afford to fall into. Falling into it could become a habit that will rob you of many things in life - happiness, health, relationship, and success. You may think that procrastination is normal and not a big deal, but if you take the time to think of the many things you can deprive yourself of because of the simple act, procrastination, you will realize it has caused a serious damage to your life that getting rid of it in the soonest possible time is vital to your total well-being.

Procrastination is not something you can't afford to ignore and as it entails the loss of everything for you - it can be a major handicap.

Here are more reasons why you should tackle procrastination before it destroys your life.

Procrastination can have its definite drawbacks.

Procrastination is a Problem Habit

This automatic and complex habit usually coexists with other negative conditions including

- Anxiety
- Organizational challenges
- Substance abuse
- Perfectionism
- Self-doubt
- Indecisiveness
- Distractibility

When occurring with other conditions, then it is in its complex form. Because it's a habit, when it coexists with other negative conditions such as negative moods, you tend to repeat this frustrating patterns of procrastination despite your awareness of its negative impact on your behavior. This is one reason why smart people keep on falling into these self-defeating patterns despite their awareness. Another reason could be non-recognition of the presence of habitual procrastination and its complexities.

It Takes Time to Focus on Ideas

When you're working on something, it takes time to focus on your ideas and more so, organize them. If you tend to do a last-minute countdown, you're sure to come up with half-baked ideas as it leaves you no time to do further research to work on major details.

You Could Have Underestimated the Time Requirement

Have you ever work on an assignment which you thought is easy enough that you set it aside for a few days and get back only when you think there's enough time to finish it? Sad to say, most of us are fond of doing this sort of thing. When we think that the job won't take much time and effort, we often set it aside in favor of a more difficult task. But what if we underestimated the time required to finish it? What if some condition arises that could impact your task?

Writers often experience this situation. An in-demand writer could have more than two assignments at a time. To be able to work on it, he decides which one he would work on first, second, and so on based on the time requirement. The time duration and the complexity of the assignment often serve as bases for weighing evaluation.

However, there are times when you fell short of the deadline because you miscalculated the proper timing. Some events or guest would surprisingly come up that would affect the time you can spend on working. An emergency perhaps can be a potential hindrance to beating last-minute deadlines. Anything can always happen, so make sure you have allocated enough time for contingencies like these.

Advantages of Living a Life Without Procrastination

When there are disadvantages to procrastination, then we must not fail to consider what we can get when we avoid procrastinating.

Most disadvantages of procrastination are preventing individuals from attaining their goals in life by diverting their focus somewhere else. By overcoming procrastination habit, we can have these benefits.

Less Work Pressure

Without this procrastination habit, working on tasks can go smoothly. The majority of people giving counsel on procrastination ends up with the time management solution. It is because time management is vital to working out procrastination habits. When you work accordingly to schedule, there will be fewer worries and less pressure. It would be somehow easy to work without your boss barking over your shoulder.

Better Job Performance

Most often, working on deadlines creates stress and pressures and end up with low-quality performance. You might have been able to finish the job on time, but it could also be below your superior's satisfaction. You fail to do your job because you did not manage your time fairly well. It is simply because of this procrastination habit that had been pestering you and affecting your performance. So, without this habit, you could expect the opposite of everything that had happened. Instead of boss unsatisfied remarks, you can expect a good performance rating and probably, a raise!

Helps Avoid Stress

When there is too much pressure in your work, it can trigger stress, anxiety, depression, and even lead to burnout! If you can overcome your procrastination habit, you can have time left for relaxation after you're done with all your responsibilities. This way, you can enjoy life. You can have more time for yourself and your family. You can live a balanced life-career lifestyle.

Chapter 2: Getting Rid of Your Procrastination Habits

Oftenpeople confused procrastination with laziness, but somehow these two are different in many aspects.

While laziness indicates an unwillingness to indulge in any activity, procrastination, on the other hand, is involved in any activity other than what should be done. In procrastination, you are trying to ignore a vital task or to delay it because you find it unpleasant. Instead of doing it immediately, you choose to do something easier and enjoyable to do. However, giving in to this trap can result in serious consequences. Procrastination can cause a decline in productivity and make you miss out your target.

When procrastination becomes such a habit, you became disillusioned and demotivated with your work which can even lead further to depression and job loss in some cases.

Recognizing When you have the Habit (Acceptance)

When you want to change a habit for the better, the first thing you need to do is to recognize its existence. It's only through the acceptance of the fact that you have this habit in you could you have the willingness to transform that habit into something that could work to your advantage.

Procrastination is an active habit

There are many reasons why you could be procrastinating, but you could be diverting your attention to a task other than the one you are scheduled to do because you have re-prioritized your workload. If you are delaying a task for some more important ones and a genuine reason, then this isn't procrastination. However putting things off indefinitely because you just avoid doing the task or simply because you switch focus, then it's procrastinating.

To be aware that you are procrastinating is vital to any changes you want to make and to be able to recognize that you have this habit in you, see if you are doing some of these:

- Start your day with a high-priority task and then do something else like taking a cup of coffee or opening your email
- Busy yourself with insignificant tasks instead of doing the most important task on your to-do list.
- You keep putting off a task that is listed on your high-priority list because you feel you are not in the mood or you keep on waiting for the right time to do it.

Exploring Possible Reasons Behind Your Procrastinations

If we take the scientific reason for procrastination, you will know that it comes from two opposing forces in our brains. One is the unconscious zone or the limbic center which includes the pleasure center. The opposing one is the prefrontal cortex; often called the internal planner.

The limbic system struggles for short-term pleasure or things we want right at this moment, while the prefrontal cortex struggles for what's best in the long run. Dr. Timothy Ph. D. who authored The Procrastinator's Digest: A Concise Guide to Solving the Procrastination Puzzle, explained that the prefrontal cortex of our brain is what separates us from animals who are controlled by the stimulus. So there's nothing automated in this weak area of our brain in contrast to the limbic system. In other words, if you want to achieve something, you need to prompt it into action intentionally.

Conversely, the limbic system does its job when we are not encouraged to take action on a certain task. This was when we gave in to procrastination.

Therefore, our procrastination is due to our biology. Economist George Ainslie could have been so right when he says that procrastination is called the basic impulse.

Paul Graham, an investor, and entrepreneur have once said that most of the impressive people he knows are terrible procrastinators. He associated it with the fact that when we do something, we tend to measure how long it will take us to finish the task. The longer it takes to be done, the less likely is the possibility of it being accomplished.

The next thing we tend to focus on is our fear when we are not sure of what will come out of something. Sometime this fear could be too great that it equates to physical pain and we are afraid it can render us into paralysis. So before it can happen, we simply pull out our handy tool for prevention - procrastination!

If we look at it this way, we can see that our brain is just trying to make some minor calculations to make life easier for us, simply for the reason that he wants you to be happy, therefore, procrastination is a defensive action provided by our natural body mechanism. But, we always look at procrastination as a bad habit, because of its eventual effect later on as we continue to procrastinate.

When there are myriads of solutions offered to us which all break down to one thing, e.g., managing time, procrastination is incurable as Paul Graham had once pointed. He likewise pointed out that procrastination is not an illness and even if how much you want to do everything, it's pointless as you can't do it. So the issue is not on how to avoid procrastination, but on how to manage it well. Procrastination and time complement each other.

We can break procrastination into three variations depending on what you want to do instead of doing what you have been thinking to do.

- You become passive
- You do something less important
- You do something more important

By simply looking at these three, you can easily pick out the most productive one who is doing the most important job at hand. However, a Professor Emeritus at Stanford, John Perry believes otherwise. According to him, by doing a less important thing, it can lead you to produce better work once you get around to doing the major ones.

Most of the procrastinators are also perfectionists so they don't do any major task when they feel they can't come with something to their satisfaction and putting it off can also be beneficial. Major ones are done only when you are inspired and in a good mood to put what you feel inside to anything that you are doing. It's the inspirational thought that triggers you to translate what you feel what you want to do. If you are in this type of mood, it is just a waste of time to spend it on something that is of less importance.

Now, that we see what's the best variant of procrastination to apply under certain time and condition, then we can be able to manage it fairly. We don't need to get ourselves controlled by a structured procrastination, but instead, we choose what's best for us under certain circumstances as long as you keep away from doing nothing at all.

Positive Procrastination

If you want procrastination to work on your side for your benefit, consider doing this.

Procrastinate on unimportant task.

Engaging in long conversations or internet surfing or doing something just to keep busy are examples of the less important tasks. Important projects need full commitment and focus. You can only have them if you have enough time and the right mood. When you are inspired to work on a major project, it would be a mistake to waste your inspiration on less important task just only because we think we should. When you want to channel your energy on important projects whenever you can, you can't devote your time to doing less important.

Structured Procrastination

This is the type of procrastination where we do less important things while we procrastinate. While we are doing the less important tasks to avoid the bigger jobs, we are tricking ourselves into accomplish some things.

When we prepare our to-do list, we put the major tasks on top as we list our tasks according to their importance. The most urgent ones usually come first. Natural procrastinators would then avoid the most important ones which are usually the difficult jobs in favor of those listed below the big ones. So, the more they avoid, the bigger jobs, the more little ones are accomplished.

Chapter 3: Implementing Strategies to Help you Manage Procrastination

For the chronic procrastinator, you must adopt some strategies to put your procrastination habit in line and get more things accomplished in less time.

Set a Goal

Behind every success is a goal. Your goal in life is what sets you apart from losers regardless of whether you will lose or gain in the end. Setting a realistic goal is what will give you the drive to move further at every point in your life. While losers simply drifted apart without any point of direction, a person with a goal moves forward towards his target and in due time reaches the point of success.

Once you set a goal to achieve, you are also presetting your success trajectory. Once it's set, nothing can stop it, but you.

Prioritize your Tasks and Responsibilities

Your workload piles up, and you have a few days to put things together. But what makes it even more impossible to beat the odds are the many urgent tasks on your to-do-list which makes it impossible for you to determine which should be on top. The result? You're getting anxious and restless that everything seems to distract you. The pressure is just too strong. It almost renders your immobility.

Time stressors could be some of the most pervasive sources of pressure in the workplace. They are triggered when there are too much to do at very little time. How can you then beat stress, and get productive in this kind of situation?

When choosing the best strategy to beat your deadlines, Eisenhower's Urgent Important Principle comes on top of the list.

Dwight D. Eisenhower, former U.S. President, categorized problems as URGENT and IMPORTANT. According to him, the urgent are not important, and the important is never urgent. With this principle, Eisenhower organized his workload.

Important tasks produced outcomes that eventually lead to the achievement of our goals. They are either personal or professional.

Urgent tasks require our immediate attention but are usually linked to achieving someone else's goal. Most of the time, we concentrated on the urgent tasks because of the urgency of the consequences of not dealing with them. When we are aware of which among our tasks are urgent and which are important, then we can prevent giving in to our natural tendency to focus on unimportant activities and secure enough time to do things that are significant to our success. This is how we can shift from a firefighting position into one where we can focus on how to be successful in our career and businesses.

Using Eisenhower's principle, list your activities, projects, assignments, tasks, and responsibilities, and then categorized them according to the following:

- Important and Urgent
- Important but not Urgent
- Not Important but Urgent
- Neither Important nor Urgent

Important and Urgent

Under this category, there are two distinct types: those you haven't anticipated, and the other one are those that you've left until the last minute. You can check out last-minute activities by planning and avoid procrastination. This one is intentional.

On the other hand, you have issues that are unforeseen or contingencies that aren't anticipated. Always make sure you have a contingency plan if a major crisis arises. You may reschedule other activities on your list. But you can only do this when you have enough time on your schedule. When you have lots of urgent and important tasks and obligations that need to be accomplished, determine which among these you could have foreseen and try next time to schedule similar activities ahead of time. This way, they won't become urgent.

Important but not Urgent

These are the task you need to focus on as they help you achieve both your personal and professional goals. Make sure that you have enough time to do these tasks perfectly especially when unforeseen issues arise out of nowhere. This will optimize your performance and chances of keeping on track.

Not Important but Urgent

Urgent but unimportant tasks often deprived you of achieving your goals. You can either delegate or reschedule these tasks. These tasks usually favored other people, and you may not want to fail them for some reason or another. This is where you must draw the line between pleasing people. You can always say "NO" when you don't want to as long as you say it politely. You may turn over the table to them so they can do it on their own.

Neither Important nor Urgent

If possible, avoid these distractions! You can ignore many of these, and they will simply fade away, but some of them could be requests from other people which you may not want to ignore. You again had to explain to them politely why you can't. When you are clear about your boundary and goals, people won't bother you with unimportant favors.

Start Small

When most of the resources about procrastination habits talk of starting with the big tasks, we can do it the other way around. Starting big is often too scary that we spend time convincing ourselves of how important it is so we can make a start. Sometimes we focus our attention on the reward so we can motivate ourselves to start working on it despite our fear and anxiety.

Working on big projects can be overwhelming and scary that we need to store up enough courage to face it, hence procrastination sets in. But this is just a matter of mindset. If you view a project as something big for you, then why not try to see in small pieces rather than the big one?

Work on the small tasks, and you will soon realize that you have completed the whole project without really being bothered by its greatness. This is how I do it every time I work on a big project that entails a long period to finish.

As a writer, we start working on the structure of the book, e.g., I would first try to picture what I would want to give the readers in the end (goal setting), and from there, I would be breaking the book into chapters and then sub chapters. I work on the most comfortable sections first, but when I'm inspired on the topic itself, I could work on the difficult chapters and easy chapters later. This way, I was able to finish the book without getting overwhelmed. The bottom line here is to work where and when you find it best. Work while in your best mood and do the ones which you can easily finish even without the drive. These are the tasks you can do which you can force yourself to do but not affecting the end-result.

There's another way to do this. Start doing small projects, so you don't need to be scared of doing something beyond your courage. As you get doing small projects, you'll soon get tired of doing something too easy. You begin to develop this drive of wanting to do more - something to level up or something that can make you prove yourself to others. As you develop this drive, your courage to venture into something new and big is likewise leveled up. You are inspired, and as inspiration takes over, that would make a great difference.

Mind Your Biggest Distractions

We are all bound to be distracted by certain things - social media, web surfing, shopping, and the usual endless chatter with colleagues. There are a lot more of these that abounds on the internet which is why online workers find time flies too fast on the web.

To avoid getting distracted especially when working on a big project, identify your biggest distractions and set it up against your priorities.

Block Apparent Distraction

When you are struggling against digital distractions, remember that there are a plethora of online tools available to temporarily block notification or websites for a certain duration of time.

As you work on your desk and set up your laptop or computer to start on your big assignment if possible, lock up your phone on your desk. A social call can abruptly up your focus from your work, and a single message can easily get you sidetracked.

Manage your mailbox and messaging tools by setting a schedule for them. Let's say you can check your mailbox in the morning before you start with your work. Try to answer only those that need an immediate response. Others can wait during lunchtime, breaks, or at night.

Other than this schedule, put your phone in a silent mode and refrain yourself from taking a peek at your social networks not unless you're working on any of these. Provide filters to your email system to avoid spams and not waste time on them.

Minimize or Block Ambient Noises

Some form of noise can shatter your concentration. Studies disclosed that ambient noise causes stress. Stress triggers the release of cortisol in your body. Cortisol is your body's automatic defense to ease the initial release of stress, but when too much of this cortisol is released, they can disrupt the prefrontal cortex or that part of the brain responsible in regulating your ability to pan and stay logical. It is also associated with your memory.

When dealing with background distractions like noises, sounds, surrounding chatters of people near you, barking dogs, etc., find a place where you can be away from these noises if you can't eliminate them. You can bring your laptop anywhere quiet and peaceful so you can focus on your work. The major point here is to avoid interruptions for when they caught you while you are in your work, it's hard to get back to focus. A few seconds of interruption will cost you an hour to refocus and regain back scattered ideas in your mind.

If you can't just leave your workplace, then invest in some noise-resistant headphones. These are likely to keep you safe from the destructive noise pollution.

Take Short Breaks

You may not want interruptions because you don't want to lose some ideas broiling in your head. Lunch is the only time you leave your desk and even rush back to work as soon as the food leaves your mouth. You may want to achieve optimal productivity, but according to a study conducted by researchers of the University of Illinois, constant work without breaks can eventually hamper concentration. Taking short breaks throughout the day can sustain your focus.

Researchers divulged that when there is constant stimulation, your brain registers it as something insignificant that it eventually clears your awareness of it. Thus, if sustained attention to a certain sensation causes it to vanish from our awareness, then for the same reason, sustained attention to a thought can lead to its disappearance in our mind! Dr. Alejandro Lleras, the leader of the team who conducted the study call this "habituation."

Habituation is like getting acclimatized to something you're doing that it loses its significance over time. Applying this to our work withers your attention to it over time. It is for this reason that we set goals along with taking frequent breaks to maintain the dedication to our project or assignment and boosts your focus until such time that you can complete the project.

Resist Devouring Big Lunches

Again, when the focus is at stake, you deprived yourself of taking breaks and so with taking snacks. Instead, you fill up your stomach by gobbling an enormous size of lunch only to slump back in your chair after your meal. Eating rich meals can fulfill your hunger, but sad to say, it dulls your mental acuity or fog your brain. You have allowed your digestive system to expend too much energy on digesting those foods you have consumed - with all those fat and carbohydrates - that it chokes the passage of your oxygen circulation leading to the brain. This impacts your ability to focus and attention on details.

To resist eating big meals on lunch hour, eat nutritious snacks during breaks especially in the morning. It stabilizes your blood sugar level and combats stomach's indulgence to heavy meals. You will notice that you will be eating less and go for a more healthier diet. This will allow you to stay sharp throughout the day.

Always Think Positive

When there's one habit, you need to develop - make that positivity. As you start acquiring a positive thinking habit, you begin to develop an optimistic point of view, and according to a research study, a positive thinking habit can make you healthier - physically, mentally, and emotionally. Positive thinking is known to improve energy and confidence. With a heightening level of self-esteem, that is sure to increase your productivity to new height levels.

To develop positivity, their tasks you need to do and here are some of them.

Face your Fears

When it comes to fear, the only way to conquer it is to repeatedly expose yourself to whatever that it is that you fear most. Research studies prove that repeated exposure reduces the psychological fear response until it moves on to being manageable until it's gone. So if you have a stage fright, conquer it by practicing giving talks in front of small groups to boosts your courage until you manage to face speaking engagements of any size.

Exposure is the most proven and effective way to deal with phobias, anxiety, and everyday fears of any types. This according to Philippe Godin a Stanford neuroscientist.

Determine the Source of Negativity

Thoughts are what feed our mind with what to do, how to react, what to say, and how to act it out. Thoughts don't come into your mind in grace or one at a time. Instead, they randomly pop out of nowhere and to keep them in control; it is necessary to monitor them.

In understanding thoughts, two mental attitudes are on demonstration: positive and negative thinking and both are rooted in invariably different causes and reasons. As negative thinking appears to be effortlessly evasive, we must be able to determine its primary causes, so we can likewise determine what triggers them to arise.

●Growing Up Years

The formative stage, e.g., childhood to adulthood has a great influence on the mental conditioning. Although there can be some transformation while you are growing up, the childhood years are very critical and can impact the thinking process of an individual.

The society and family are the primary factors that largely influence the change in an individual. Hence, if the individual exposure comprises more of unpleasant events and situations, these bad and hurting memories are more embedded in the mind and conditioning it to view things more in the negative light. As that person grows into maturity, it hurts his self-esteem and causes him to lose his self-confidence and assertiveness, but there are individuals who cope up with their situation and manage to reverse its effects on their lives.

If you realize that you have this pessimistic attitude, try looking back to your childhood days and determine what events had contributed to the development of negativism in your attitude. Who are the people who have contributed to the formation of these negative thoughts? Try to go back and see the positive side of it. You may even be surprised to see that they are not as bad as the way you thought they are at that time.

In a family set-up where the exchange of harsh words and statement were but a natural day occurrence, the effect on the children is the development of a negative outlook in life, and as they grow up, these children will tend to manifest a similar mindset.

●Depressing and Traumatic Incidents in life

Traumatic life experiences trigger depression, and the person who had undergone such traumatic experience can easily associate it with negative thoughts. When flashbacks of those distressing events can bring pain and unpleasant memories, vivid pictures of these memories can come back to life to remind the person of the debilitating event. That individual would then easily succumb to the feeling of hatred and worthlessness and easily falls into the pit of negativity. If you are this individual, you may look at life as a complete misfortune, and you believe that nothing good can come out of life anymore.

●Negative Thinking Patterns

When you have very low self-esteem as a result of negativity, it is largely due to negative thinking patterns inherent in every individual. There are many kinds of distorted cognitive behaviors which may or may not be manifested in an individual. Sometimes, you will only realize that you are reflecting negative thinking patterns because other people will tell you. These people recognize them are these are evident in your actions, words, expressions or non-verbal cues.

A common example would be your way of forecasting a trouble or mess even before it happens. These are false assumptions of the outcome of some actions of course. You tend to prejudge people and events in the negative light which somehow lead you to develop a pattern of negative thinking - a negative mental behavior. When you choose to see the negative point of view of almost everything, this is an example of what we have referred here as cognitive distortion.

Negative thinking could not only weaken the mind. It likewise weakens the heart for when negative thoughts creep into our nerves; it impacts your feelings and convictions. Therefore, you need to be more keen on identifying the sources of your negative thinking to find ways to combat it.

When you're thinking of a bad situation or when an issue suddenly arises which left you unguarded so that negative thoughts start to crop, counteract by asking yourself positive questions. These questions should help you feel better and useful for you to learn so you can have this chance to grow and develop.

Here are sample questions you may ask yourself.

- What can I earn from this situation?
- Is there something good about this?
- Can my family, friends or relatives help me in this situation?
- Can I do anything to get a better result out of this?

Get Rid of Mental Clutter

Do you think that your brain could be working against you? This sounds weird, but this could happen to all of us at one time or another. When I got my mind clogged with confusion, anxiety, and indecisiveness, I find myself battling with my mind. I just could not decide what to do, and I'm drained of my energy to think logically.

Let's say I have a hard time at work. A client keeps on requesting for some revisions on some portion of the article that were not even included in the agreement when I started working on it. I don't want to give in, but I don't feel I have the energy to win the battle.

There's something that's even worse than having cluttered surroundings - home or workspace, and that's it has a cluttered mind. Mental clutter moves in various directions at once, and that's what keeps us from finishing our tasks. We tend to think of too many things a that we end up with no result at all. All we ever manage to accomplish are dwellings on insignificant matters.

Mental clutter is the bundle of worries you have that gets you restless and out of focus. It includes worrying about what will the future brings and ruminating about something tragic that happened in the past. An empty run of a to-do-list keeps hanging on your mind leaving you mentally fatigued and physically drained.

Luckily, strategies and techniques were introduced so you can clean out some space in your mind. Here are some of them.

- **Declutter your Surroundings**

The physical clutter may not equal mental clutter, but still, it can always lead to it. Note that clutter bombards your mind excessively with stimuli that force the brain to work harder. When there is the presence of physical clutter surrounding you, it automatically sends the signal to the brain that something else needs to be done or fixed. Thinking of it alone can exhaust you mentally.

By declutterring your surrounding, you will discover that your mind is likewise de-cluttered. Removing the stimuli that trigger the brain on red alert puts the brain at ease and peace with its surroundings.

- **Write It Down**

Most of us are fond of storing everything in our brain. To stop cogging your memory with unnecessary things, use a tool for storing those bits of information which you need to remembers. This too can be an app or any online too. It can also be a piece of paper or journal. You may use these tools to write down your appointments, important dates and events, phone numbers and any ideas you can use for future projects.

Keeping a journal is also writing important facts but with more depth, as it allows you to scribble an inner chatter that constantly interrupts your thoughts when some tasks need to be done.

A Writing in a journal could include any or of the following:

- Things that give you worries.
- Plans for achieving something like a goal.
- Concerns about something - health or relationship that's draining you of your energy.

There are a lot more of things you can include in your journal.

- **Let Go of Something in the Past**

Mind clutter is often related to something which happened in the past. Unknowingly, we keep a huge cabinet of mental drawers at the back of our minds. These drawers are linking us back to our past. They are filled with mistakes, failures, missed opportunities, bitterness grievances, and much more.

Take time to evaluate what fill up your mental draw and try discarding every content until you have thoroughly clean them up. Memories of the past that aren't serving you we need to go so they can't serve as the cutter to your present life.

- **Stop Multitasking**

Most often, we love to do things simultaneously which cause us to lose focus on the significant ones. Freelancers often do this kind of thing. They do this on purpose to get more things done and to get away with the boredom of concentrating just on one task. There are people who have mastered the art of multitasking. They can retain their focus even while working on 2-3 jobs at a time because they have been used to doing it. It has become a habit for them. However, it is not recommended that you do the same. It's always better to concentrate doing one thing at a time. This way, you will not be compromising your performance.

- **Limit the Amount of Incoming Information**

Too much information stored in your brain can likewise cog your memory. Because of the advancement in technology, we can't help but be bombarded with new and current events, social media, entertainments, and much more. Our devices-phones, tablets, laptops, TVs, and desktops are full of this massive information that we need to limit them if we want to have our brain functioning we.

Limit this information and create space by simply doing the following:

- Set a limit on the time you allocate each day for browsing the internet outside of research works relevant to your project.
- Unsubscribe from any websites that aren't contributing to your quality of life but are in fact provide distractions to your work.
- Pay attention only to credible sources of information.
- Determine the relevance of information sources and discard those that aren't relevant to your success.

- **Be Decisive**

If your mailbox is filled with messages, but you aren't doing anything about it, soon it will be overflowing with messages, requests, bills, and so on. The way to clear it is to make your decision of what to do with each item. Start by using filters, so you don't have to deal with spam. Then decide which ones need no answer, and which ones do. Quickly deletes or archives those you don't need to answer. For the rest, decide on their urgency, importance, and significance.

The same thing applies to your brain. If you put off making decisions, it will soon be cluttered with undecided matters. The solution, therefore, is to be decisive.

- **Run Routine Decisions on Auto-Pilot**

Small, routine tasks can take a lot of brain space. Things like what to eat for breakfast, what to wear, what show to watch for tonight, etc.

You can reduce the amount of brain space by making a scheduled habit of doing things like:

Prepare to an omelet for Monday morning breakfast, beef steak for lunch, and so on. Likewise, wear a blue polo with black pants every Tuesday, and watch a certain movie show on its scheduled day.

- **Prioritize**

Of course, you have your to-do-list to follow every day. But if you keep adding more to the list while reducing your time doing what's in there, then you come up with a list of accumulating undone tasks. This is where prioritizing is needed. Do what you consider best according to what you learned from here and apply it. See what will happen.

Mental clutter leads to a congestion of your brain. It hinders you from having a clear view of things and takes your focus away from what matters. Declutter your mind, and you will immediately see clearly what's need to be done first.

Don't Try Pleasing People

People pleasing is frequently based on perfectionism because without getting any positive feedback from other people of how beautiful, smart, organized, or practically perfect they are, they feel they are NOTHING! As we have previously discussed, perfectionism has always been one of the major causes of procrastination, and while we are closely investigating the relationship between people pleasing and perfectionism, we can see that they have many things in common which make them both influencing factors for procrastination.

Perfectionists and people pleasing often look to their peers for approval. This outward display of approval is fulfilling for a while but becomes void in the long run. Since this approval does not come from the inside, these type of persons can't truly feel the depth of people's acceptance. And so for this reason, without that constant declaration of acceptance and display of approval, their self-worth and self-esteem waver.

There is so much hanging on other people's acceptance as they fear to be rejected to the extent that they need to sacrifice for others. Everything about them is a denial and a betrayal of their self-worth which eventually result in a wide range of negative emotions - bitterness, anger, hatred, jealousy, shattered self-confidence. Sometimes, they could end up to be violent if not prone to suicide attempts.

People pleaser procrastinates as they tend to do first what others ask of them and these are usually not on their to-do-list. Favors ask just come out of the blue, and a people pleaser doesn't have the sense to reject anyone that comes asking for favor or help. For them, it's always an opportunity to grab as it equates to another entry on his validation record.

When anyone could just come and asks for anything, a people pleaser own set of tasks are then pushed on the backseat. Because his reason for doing these services are not truly fulfilling him inwardly as he doesn't enjoy doing them, he ends up drained of energy.

Prioritizing other people's goal is inherent in a people pleaser, and that life has become an agony despite those efforts of pleasing others just to gain acceptance. This is a psychological order that needs to be given attention, and it's not enough that we deal with the procrastination issue here, but you can always start by learning to say, "NO" when things got in your way.

If you are a people pleaser, you must remember that you can't please people at all times. Even if you have provided them favors too many time, and you failed them once, that one time will always be remembered. Learn to love yourself and others will love you for what you are. It never pays to hate yourself and expects others to love and accept you. Loving starts from within yourself before it will reflect others.

Learn Meditation Exercises

When our days are filled with our busy obligations and an unending list of tasks that need to be accomplished, we easily forget that we are uniquely brilliant and courageous individuals trying to create something that we only can create. Many obstacles get in our way, bringing us to a slow crawl or eventually stop us from achieving what we want to achieve.

There are times when you begin moving aimlessly as the future looks bleak, but as there's no point of return, you need to stop there and then. This temporary halt in your activities is just to take a breath from life's complexity - to take a break and reset as well as refocus the mind so you can continue to move on while in this fast-paced world.

This temporary pause is what we do to meditate. For less than an hour of your time, take time to be with yourself. Seek refuge in a peaceful place or if you can manage to be alone with yourself even with other people surrounding you, do some simple meditation exercises. Start with the breathing exercise. It's as simple as breathing in and breathing out. The only difference is the concentration while feeling the slow movement of your breath as it goes in and out of your body. Meditation can provide you with a clearer view of what's happening at present and teach you to how to block external distractions. Inner distractions are likewise released through meditation.

Visualize Success

Fantasizing about the future is alright right but fantasizing excessively can also be a goal killer and a good reason for many people to procrastinate.

A study on motivation and fantasies reveals that when you build castles in the sky, that can be destructive to real and attainable goals. Participants of the study were tested to determine how commonplace fantasizing about future and were followed up with their performance in various categories.

Participants were subject to job searches. The study revealed that those who spent more time dreaming about getting a job are worst on their performance and two years after college, these dreamers:

- Applied for fewer jobs
- They offered fewer jobs
- And for those working, they are not sufficiently paid.

Well, this isn't nice to hear! As we all know, positive visualizations can stimulate us to drive ourselves much further. So, what seems to be wrong here?

According to this study from UCLA, the error lies in what we visualize.

The study disclosed that those participants who included in their visualization the process of what's needed to be done to achieve the goal are more likely to perform well. Example of this is when you visualize to become a successful businessman and every day you visualize that you are conducting business in your office.

There are two reasons for the visualization to work more likely.

Planning: When you visualize the process, these help focus attention on the steps needed to reach the goal.

Emotion: Visualization of individual steps can lead to the reduction of anxiety.

So don't worry about your dreams, but rather focus on its achievement and remember to include the steps necessary to realize your dream!

Improve Lifestyle

When you have trouble living with your procrastination issue, then it's time that you make a shift to your lifestyle to improve it. Procrastination does not only involves one habit that you can change. In fact, procrastination works in integrated patterns connecting one issue to another. It is a summary of life's choices that eventually lead up to one common system - PROCRASTINATION!

We often procrastinate because we are either physically or emotionally drained to work. When you fall into such pattern, you can feel lazy because your energy level is too low that doing even just a simple task seems too much work for you. You can't blame the task for being tedious. It's just that you conserve energy, so you procrastinate. But the longer you do it this way, the more that your procrastination habit is spiraling towards depression. Feeling unmotivated and weak must not become your norm, so try to disrupt this pattern as you become aware of its occurrence.

Have a Regular Exercise

For a straightforward solution, you need to move to get out of the inertia. Move your legs, your arms, your butt, and your whole body! When you allow your energy to soar up, you will be less resistant to movement, and any task will be much easier. A person in good fit can handle more activity regardless of whether the task is hard or easy to manage.

Eat a Healthy Diet

Exercise must go with a proper and healthy diet to keep your energy consistently high. When your energy is high, you feel too alive to let the day passed without anything to do because you have a clear mind and well-fueled body to take your tasks for the day.

Consuming raw fruits and vegetables along with enough content of protein and carbohydrates can fully energize your body. Fruits and vegetables are also good sources of antioxidants to keep your body free from any form of natural contaminants. Once your digestive system is unclogged, your body metabolism improves and so is your health.

Practice Early-to-Bed and Early-to-Rise Habit

Having enough quality sleep and relaxation will not only increase your energy level but likewise improve your mental clarity and heightens your cognitive functioning ability.

When you sleep early, you wake up early. When you wake up early to greet the morning sun, you get most of the positive energy from the greatest source of light. This could be the reason why when you wake up early, you are in a better mood, feels energetic, and ready to face every change that comes your way.

Chapter 4: Even Winners Procrastinate!

It might surprise you to know that even successful people like Bill Clinton, Douglas Adams, Margaret Atwood, Frank Lloyd Wright, Victor Hugo, Leonardo da Vinci, and Mariah Carey are all known for their last-minute-craps. Wrights Architectural masterpiece, *Falling water* was reportedly drawn 30 minutes before the arrival of his client.

Negative as it may appear to you, procrastination, seems to have been mastered by these super-rich influencers in their industry had effectively utilized it as a tool for working their advantage.

Successful people attain their success being a massive taskmaster, but as success entails more responsibilities, it likewise dilutes their priorities. Of course, they continue believing that accomplishing more is best, but then they also now have their attention shift to more urgent tasks and placing more significant goals on standby.

In simple terms, these successful people are purposely procrastinating! However, when they do this on purpose, they are solving the priority dilution issue. Instead of accomplishing tasks listed on a to-do-list, they subject each task through a focus change while asking themselves the following questions.

- Can I just ignore this task?
- Can I subject this task to automation?
- Can I delegate this task to another person?

If the task can't be done through these three process then the final question would be:

- Can it wait until later?

If it is urgent and must be done immediately, then get rid of all forms of distractions by:

- Shutting your phone off
- Closing the door
- Posting a message of "DON'T DISTURB" outside your door.

If it's an urgent matter, then you must do it now, but if not, then it's best to procrastinate on purpose so you can give your time and focus on finishing more significant tasks on hand.

The best illustration for putting off a task on purpose is when you book your flight. Booking a flight earlier than scheduled is good. Others are doing it six months earlier. Even if you think it's best to book early, still it is sensible to wait and book it when it's near the scheduled time. Everything is changing, so if something arises which needs a change in your scheduled fight, then you need to reschedule it. When you do, you will be investing more time and money changing what you have previously booked.

These successful people understand the risk of being late, but they also understand that being too early sometimes entails a risk than they can surely avoid by using a bit of sensibility.

You can make procrastinating on purpose a strategic advantage to work for you. As you put a task through the focus funnel, it is important that you understand the difference between important, significance, and urgent.

- Important is how much a task matters.
- Significant is how long a task matters.
- Urgent is how soon a task matters.

Successful people are winners, and they often live under urgency. They often focus on significant tasks and invest more time into things that pay off in the long run. Winners know exactly how to choose a task they need to focus on, and they know that it's not just about today. They intentionally choose the ones that create a better tomorrow.

Success is not all about volume. There is a big difference in not doing a task simply for the reason that you don't feel like doing it, and not doing the task because you know this is not the best time to do it. Waiting on purpose is not about being lazy to do something. Waiting on purpose is waiting patiently because you know that by doing so, you can achieve something out of it. Successful men have mastered their timing, and that's what makes them a true WINNER!

Chapter 5: Resource Tools to Help Manage Your Tasks and Time

People who are success-oriented are always in a hurry and seem to be running out of time. If you are one of them, then you need to concern with finding out on how to maximize your performance with limited time resources.

Time is so vast, and yet it is running in limited resources, and you can't afford to waste even just a fraction of it. You need to do everything to manage it well - from scheduling meetings up to fulfilling the orders as time is significant in every aspect of the business.

Ineffective time management can be displayed in many forms - procrastination, distractions, or assignments that take more time than they should. There are tons of ways to waste time and wasted time always ended up in rushed deadlines, added stress and anxiety, and an overall imbalance in life and work.

When it happens, you can't add more time to what you already have, but you can use the time that you have more efficiently. Luckily, we have more tools and time management apps that can help us find time to create a life-work balance and optimal performance.

Clear

Clear is a simple, to-do-list app designed to efficiently help you accomplish your tasks and be in full control of your time and day. By using a themed list, you can be able to organize your tasks into separate categories as it gives you an outlook on what you need to do next. Regardless of how busy you can be with your schedule, the app is most likely to help you view your goal more objectively.

Clear's greatest feature lies on its easy interface while it gives you a full hand for customizing your settings. By simply using gesture, you can quickly add and complete tasks without much ado. You can avail of Cedar for iOS, OS X, and Apple Watch.

Added Features

This app syncs with your account, thereby, eliminating the need for a regular updating of your to-do-list on your devices every time you complete a task.

Keeps you accountable for push notifications and reminders that requires you not to overlook what needs to be done.

Workflow

When you think you just don't have much time, this highly customizable app shaves time off the complicated things you do every day. With this app, you can perform batches of tasks in just a single click by creating unique home screen shortcuts on your phone. If you need a Google map to provide directions for your next meeting or backup roll photos on your Dropbox, you can customize this app to take care of your every need.

Workflow prided itself on over 200 features and integration with social media apps like YouTube, Facebook, and Uber. Workflow is available for iOS. This app can likewise operate inside other apps including Safari and Evernote.

Clara

This artificial intelligent email app does more than scheduling and coordinating your meetings. When booking meetings can be tough, Clara takes the legwork out of arranging meetings by automatically handling the tedious task of sending and receiving emails every day that makes you waste so much time.

Simply furnish Clara with a copy of any email and the app will start the process of setting up a meeting in a short time.

Clara is reliable when it comes to freeing up your mailbox and reduce your time spent on sending emails. It also lets you focus on completing the task instead of having to worry about the schedule. To top it all, with Clara, you feel like you're dealing with a real person as it interacts with a natural language capability that truly won't confuse recipients of messages.

Wunderlist

This is a collaborative app designed to solve the issue with time as it helps you coordinate with your friends, family, and co-workers.

When you intend to get things done, Wunderlist assists you in tracking, completing, and sharing your goals with just a single click. You can assign tasks, set due dates, and add comments along with reminders for your collaborating tasks. Wunderlist is available for Android, iOS, Windows Phone, OS X, and Windows as well as Google Chrome.

Added Features

Wunderlist works on almost every platform - devices for collaborating tasks and constantly reminds you of dates and schedule so you won't be missing anything that needs to be done.

Google Now

This is a management app that serves as an intelligent voice-powered assistant. It processes a complicated request by simply using your behavior to anticipate the kind of information that you' need even before your asking.

With Google's wide range of data to support it, Google can now be preemptive to serve you with the information that could be more relevant to your needs. From just anything you need to anything under the sun, Google now can free up your time while taking care of the little things for you.

This Google app is also integrated with other Google applications and allows you to do more tasks making one's life more convenient despite busy days.

Available in Android and iOS, Google Now allows you to have more focus on your work by giving you more information without the need to dive into a search result.

Google Now app automatically adapts to your behavior to give you a uniquely amazing and customized experience that can quickly make a shift as you do.

Pocket

This bookmarking app allows you to save articles for reading later. Even during the productive period, you can easily be thrown off the track when you suddenly come across a fascinating content. To avoid this, Pocket lets you save these interesting piece at one place so you can get back to it later when you're done with your work.

Pocket works with more than 1500 apps so you can save content for later use regardless of where you find them. The app is available for both Android and iOS. So what more can Pocket app do for you?

Pocket helps you organize your time by separating working hours from learning hours. Pocket also makes it easier for you to discover a new content, so when it's time for your learning, there is no shortage of materials.

Chapter 6: 10-Minute Exercise of Breaking the Habit (Transforming or Replacement of Habits)

Now that we have learned a lot about procrastination, its effects, and causes and how we can learn from other people's experiences, it's time that we apply what we have learned to our own life. When procrastination seems to be a habit, then it may take time to dispose of them completely, but while you are trying to do just that, we can gradually disengage yourself from these automated routines by adopting a more positive habit to replace the old ones.

Bad habits are hard to break, but it doesn't seem impossible to do so. When it's rooted in our inner senses or system, then we can uproot these habits slowly and change them with positive ones - those that are useful and contribute to our success and happiness in life.

If you need to do something now within 10 minutes that could be useful to you for the rest of your life, what would that be?

Here are some exercises which you can accomplish within 10 minutes but its effects could last you a lifetime as it will help you get rid of your procrastination habit.

Step #1 - Track your Daily Activities

As you start doing this, you feel that it's just a waste of time, but you will be surprised to realize afterward - let's say when you have gathered a month's data - the reason why there seems to be not enough time to do necessary tasks and activities. This exercise will help you identify habits that are created over time.

Most of us are spending a majority of their time indulging in social media networks - browsing, chatting, exchanging emails, and even bashing other Netizens as they got carried away reading shared posts. Clicking one post could lead to another until you are trapped in the web and out of your schedule and direction. Once you get into your Facebook account, you can't help watching videos that can lead you to visit another site and so on.

If you became aware of the specific activities that are keys to bringing you procrastination habits, then you can start avoiding them and go directly to the tasks on your to-do list.

Step #2 - Rid Yourself of Distraction

When it seems impossible to focus on what you want to do because of your phone's ringing or notification alerts, then start by keeping yourself free from this distraction.

Turn off your phone and keep it away from view. Set it to the silent mode and check your mailbox only before you leave the house, at break time, and after arriving home from work or before you go to sleep.

Maintain a notepad on your computer especially when you're working on it. Whenever some random idea strikes, don't rush to search it online unless you're working on that certain topic. Instead, record it in notepad when you do your research later.

Step #3 - Set Deadlines

Get into the habit of disciplining yourself. Set a deadline to complete a task and motivate yourself to focus on it.

Before I'm through with an assignment, I start working on another one. This motivates me to beat the deadline so I can work full-time on the other topic. Besides, it saves me from the monotony working on a single project. So the more projects I have, the more motivated I get to work on it. The challenge of working on more than one project at a time keeps me from deviating my attention to another task that is less than significant, urgent or important.

Step #4 - Transform a Habit

Understanding the Power of Habit as an introduced principle by Charles Duhigg can help. According to him, a habit involves a cycle of cue (Signal), routine, and Reward. This simply means that a habit is automated as is embedded in your senses. You do a routine task without really thinking of it because it has been with you for a long time that you get used to it. But a habit is triggered by a certain cue or signal which set it on automation and to set up a habit; it involves reward so you can have the motivation to get back doing it.

To illustrate, I have this habit of not being able to sleep at night. As a writer, I often stay late to write my assignments until I get used to it. To break this habit, I start watching a movie via YouTube in bed at night. Before I could reach the middle of the movie, I'm fast asleep.

He cue here is the bed and the film. The bed alone or the film alone is not enough to get me to sleep, but when both are present, I have this reward of a good night's sleep which is rewarding for me because I have this chronic insomnia.

If you have some habit to change and you need to replace it with a better one. Always look for the cue. Avoid the cue for the old habit that needs breaking and set up the cue for the new habit. After you determine the cue, starts exercising it daily to include it in your routine task, and every time you do, reward yourself for a good job.

Step #5 - Sustaining the Habits

When you are successful with the new habit that keeps you away from procrastinating, be consistent and keep on improving by doing the following:

- **Track your Activities:** Don't forget to list down what you have done for the day and analyze what you do to do better the next day.
- **Prioritize Activities for Tomorrow**: When you have a summary of your activities, it helps you decide what tasks should be placed on top of your to-do-list. Be sure don't put enough tasks that could get you busy for more than a day.

These 10-minute habit-forming activities need to be monitored for consistency. To do this, consider exercising the following:

- **Set a Monthly Review:** To improve more on your productivity and get rid of your procrastination habits, review your collected data every month and see which habits need to go. Also, evaluate the success of the new habits. Are you consistent with these new habits you acquired? If not, then you have to begin all over again.

Chapter 7: Success Stories

Every one of us procrastinates. Even successful and super-rich individuals struggle with it every day, but they do something most of us ordinary people don't - they move past their procrastinating habit. They don't justify or allow procrastination to affect their end-result.

Here are some prominent individuals whose lives are filled with procrastinating days. Some did something to get rid of them, some live with them, and some are forced to keep up with them. What's common, they are great procrastinators, yet, they succeed regardless of the intensity of its effects on their lives.

Dalai Lama

The 14th Dalai Lama, Tenzin Gyatso is a great spiritual leader and advocate for the Tibetan people. He had been traveling the world teaching about happiness and compassion. As a student, Gyatso was a bored youngster and not easy to be motivated. According to him, it was only in the face of challenge and urgent deadlines that he would be forced to study. These had served him his lessons, and now his teachings include anti-procrastination practices.

"Rather should you make preparations so even when you die tonight, then you don't have any regrets."

-- Dalai Lama

Victor Hugo

This French novelist and poet are serious in dealing with his procrastinate habit that he found a unique way to get rid of it. He would have his servant stripped him naked in this study and would not allow him to return with his clothes until he was done with the appointed task. Epic historical novels authored by Victor Hugo include Les Miserables and the Hunchback of Notre Dame.

Herman Melville

This American author procrastinating habit had reached its peak that he had to ask his wife to bound him in a manner that he won't be able to leave his deck while he was writing his epic novel, Moby Dick also named The Whale. Despite this extreme way of combating procrastination, he earned his reward as his book was named among the greatest fiction books ever written.

Frank Lloyd Wright

The great American architect is famous for his last-minute work of art, the *Falling water*, a house in rural Pennsylvania in 1964 which he finished within two hours of rushed work at the age of 67.

Edgar Kaufmann, a wealthy businessman from Pittsburg, contracted the architect to design the *Falling water* but after his visit to the site, procrastination took the best of him, and he never drew a thing until he received a call from Kauffman early Sunday morning telling him that he would be checking on him before lunch to see the design.

This could have sent an ordinary procrastinator to panic, but Wright calmly finished his breakfast and started drawing the plan in front of anxious apprentices. He was able to finish it just before Kauffman entered his office.

Falling water was included among Smithsonian's life list of 28 popular places you need to see before you die. The masterpiece was likewise listed as a National Historic landmark in 1966.

The famous American architect was not only a master of his craft but had also mastered over procrastination and reversing its effect to his full advantage.

Margaret Atwood

Canada's one prolific and celebrated writer, Margaret Atwood prided herself of overcoming procrastination when during her five decades of writing and establishing a career which stretched back to 1961, she had written 14 novels, 16 volumes of poetry, 9 short story collections, 8 children books, 10-full length non-fiction works, 4 e-Books, 3 TV scripts, and two librettos.

According to this great author, she spends her mornings worrying and procrastinating and then plunges into a frenzied attack of anxiety while waiting at around 3:00 p.m.

Bill Clinton

Tagged as a chronic procrastinator by Time Magazine, the former U.S. President was a real example of it. It was reportedly said that his aides would give the former president long periods than necessary just to review and make comments on early drafts of significant speeches. However, everything would end up as it usually did - last-minute cut-and-paste revisions. Hilary, his wife reportedly admitted that it was indeed maddening trying to keep him on schedule.

Leonardo da Vinci

Known today as the genius of the Renaissance period, Leonardo da Vinci had also got this reputation as a daydreamer that accomplished nothing before he had risen into popularity because of his masterpieces in arts. He is no doubt a man who is incredibly talented and had explored every field of Science and Arts - Engineering, Anatomy, Botany, Biology, Architecture, Mathematics, and Physics. Aside from painting where he became famous, he was also into sculpting and drawing plans for ingenious machines that are significant to the future including airplanes, helicopters, and submarines. But his procrastination habit became his greatest disadvantage as he never managed to finish a project on time.

Leonardo can be distracted by anything. This was what wasted his energy and talents. Even his famous work of art, the Mona Lisa took 16 years to complete. It also took him 13 years to finish the version of the Virgin of the Rocks now displayed in London's National Gallery. His other works including Jerome in the Wilderness and The Adoration of Magi were never finished along with his equestrian projects that were never built.

The famous painting of the Last Supper was evidence of the painter's procrastinating habit. The Duke of Milan, his patron, had gone to the extent of threatening Leonardo with a fund cut off before he finally succeeded completing the project.

Even the famous painting of The Last Supper only completed after his patron, Ludovico Sforza, Duke of Milan threatened a fund cut off. In his later years, Leonardo regrets are said to include never having completed a single work that he appealed to God to tell him if anything has been done".

Samuel Taylor Coleridge

A famous English Poet of the 18th century, Coleridge was likewise famous for his being a procrastinator. During his lifetime, publishers were constantly reporting of forthcoming pieces of works that never came to reality. The works he left were in fragments, brilliantly made but were void of competition.

Molly Lefebure, author of the Book, A Bondage of Opium depicted Coleridge miserable life and unending sufferings.

Just like many of our known procrastinators, Coleridge was also an impulsive person influenced by his passions for the moment which was constantly interrupting him from accomplishing his long-term goal. And because Coleridge was addicted to opium, this even enhanced his impulsiveness and made matters worst to the extent that it provided a powerful source of distraction. He was always caught between choosing whether to smoke opium or finish his work. Most often, opium won out.

Kublai Khan, his famous poem was never finished, and the poet contended that it was an opium-inspired dream that was interrupted.

Douglas Adam, the author of the Hitchhiker's Guide to the Galaxy was famous for this being a procrastinator as he was for his "I love deadlines!" one-liner. Despite his procrastination, he managed to write nine books though he declared his aversion to writing. He would put off a task by spending his day in bed, taking a bath or drinking cups of tea. He needed his publishers and editors to lock him up in his room and glowered at him until he starts working just to overcome his procrastination. His friend Steve Meretzky testified that this isn't an exaggeration for Adam's procrastination has become a form of art for him. The Hitchhiker's guide would never have been done if Steve hadn't gone over to England and threaten him to camp out on his doorsteps.

Though Adam was a great writer, his procrastination seemed to stem out of his aversion to writing. He never likes paper and pen that he put his writing off until there was an urgency for its need. Adam struggled to finish his final novel, The Salmon of Doubt that he would rather soak in the bath for long hours just to avoid doing it. He had worked on it for ten years and still was not able to finish the first draft when a heart attack struck him dead. Pieces of this novel were published posthumously but were rather incomprehensible for a novel.

General George McClellan

General McClellan over-cautiousness to fight when he felt that the odds are against him or when he is not sure that they can win the battle. The North could have won the war a lot faster if the General did not procrastinate. He was known for his being meticulous especially in preparing the Union Army, but his endless preparation could be a form of his procrastination.

Former President, Abraham Lincoln never doubted the General excellent performance in the Civil War. He said that if the general can't fight himself, he excels in making others ready to fight, except that when the chips were down, the general couldn't bring himself to go to the battlefield.

Because of this procrastination, the general missed his opportunity to capture Richmond from Robert E. Lee's men. Also in the same year, it took him too much time to make decisions before and after the battle of Antietam, wasting what could have been his great advantages over Lee and this cause the war to drag to an extra three year.

Conclusion

Procrastination has always been a part of one's lifestyle. Either you want to get ahead of others, or you want to be the last one to finish, it doesn't matter as long as you produce results to your satisfaction. Just like other influencing factors in our life, procrastinating has its positive and negative sides, and what matters most is how you use procrastination to your advantage. It's on how you look at procrastination that makes the difference. It can be your weakness, or it can be your strength, and people who can master over their procrastination habit came out to be more successful than those who just want to get rid of them.

How you manage your procrastination habit is a choice just as life is filled up with choices. Every individual is unique in their way that one strategy of resolving the procrastination issue may not be possible for another, though of course, we have general guidelines to start with. All depends on how you understand yourself well and how you spend time analyzing your behavior, attitude, habits, character, personality. No one could know you better more than you do.

Procrastination issue exists for a reason. Try to explore your life deeper to determine what had caused you to procrastinate. When you learn to understand yourself more clearly and with depth, you can do some tweaking to make your procrastination habit works for you instead of getting depressed.

If you noticed in the last chapter, we have included success stories of prominent personalities with procrastination habits. This is to show you the significance of procrastination is significant to success. However, I would like to point out the fact that some of these personalities never live a happy life. It is because, regardless of the success they have, even until the end, they did not recognize the advantage of procrastination.

Procrastination may not be the real issue here, but is just a symptom of an underlying physical or psychological disorder that needs to be further probed into. But regardless of what it is, the fact that you need to reverse its negative effects and optimize the positive ones to your full advantage is what matters!

www.ingramcontent.com/pod-product-compliance
Lightning Source LLC
Chambersburg PA
CBHW051330220526
45468CB00004B/1577